Get A Handle On Life

GET A HANDLE ON PROCRASTINATION

MONIQUE JOINER SIEDLAK

Oshun
Publications

Get a Handle on Procrastination © Copyright 2021 by Monique Joiner Siedlak

ISBN: 978-1-950378-57-9

All rights reserved

The content contained within this book may not be reproduced, duplicated or transmitted without direct written permission from the author or the publisher.

Under no circumstances will any blame or legal responsibility be held against the publisher, or author, for any damages, reparation, or monetary loss due to the information contained within this book, either directly or indirectly.

Legal Notice

This book is copyright protected. It is only for personal use. You cannot amend, distribute, sell, use, quote or paraphrase any part, or the content within this book, without the consent of the author or publisher.

Disclaimer Notice

Please note the information contained within this document is for educational and entertainment purposes only. All effort has been executed to present accurate, up to date, reliable, complete information. No warranties of any kind are declared or implied. Readers acknowledge that the author is not engaged in the rendering of legal, financial, medical or professional advice. The content within this book has been derived from various sources. Please consult a licensed professional before attempting any techniques outlined in this book.

By reading this document, the reader agrees that under no circumstances is the author responsible for any losses, direct or indirect, that are incurred as a result of the use of the information contained within this document, including, but not limited to, errors, omissions, or inaccuracies.

Cover Design by MJS

Cover Image by gstockstudio@depositphotos.com

Published by Oshun Publications

www.oshunpublications.com

CONTENTS

Other Books in Series	v
A Great Offer	vii
Introduction	xi
1. What Is Procrastination?	1
2. Reasons for Procrastination	7
3. Use Parkinson's Law	17
4. Eat the Frog First	21
5. Prioritize Your Tasks and Projects	27
6. Take Small Bites	33
7. When Someone Else Set Your Deadlines	37
8. Be Accountable to Someone	41
9. Remove Digital and Environmental Distractions	45
10. Focus on One Task at a Time	51
11. Incentives to Give Yourself	57
12. Perform a Weekly Checkup of Your Goals	61
13. Don't Be Hard on Yourself if You Fail	65
Conclusion	69
References	75
About the Author	77
Other Series by Monique	79
Last Chance	81
Thank You!	83

OTHER BOOKS IN SERIES

Get a Handle on Life
    Get a Handle on Anxiety
    Get a Handle on Depression

Want to learn about African Magic, Wicca, or even Reiki while cleaning your home, exercising, or driving to work? I know it's tough these days to simply find the time to relax and curl up with a good book. This is why I'm delighted to share that I have books available in audiobook format.

Best of all, you can get the audiobook version of this book or any other book by me for free as part of a 30-day Audible trial.

Members get free audiobooks every month and exclusive discounts. It's an excellent way to explore and determine if audiobook learning works for you.

If you're not satisfied, you can cancel anytime within the

trial period. You won't be charged, and you can still keep your book. To choose your free audiobook, visit:

www.mojosiedlak.com/free-audiobooks

INTRODUCTION

Since you are human, you probably have hit the snooze button at least once in your life. Come on; admit it—you know you have. It's such a simple action and one we usually wouldn't give a second thought to. After all, none of us are perfect, and we have all given in to the temptation of sleeping for just ten more minutes. Perhaps it happens more often than we would like to admit. Performed once in a while, hitting the snooze button is nothing to worry about. However, for many, this is a typical morning routine and a real example of the art of procrastination.

Don't be alarmed (no pun intended) because if this is indeed a routine habit for you, there is a simple fix. After all, the morning is an essential part of your day, so why sleep in and waste those minutes? So, take the initiative. Don't hit that snooze button, and begin to change the way you treat your mornings. You might be surprised by how making one simple adjustment to this habit can change the way your day turns out. So, awaken to another glorious morning, and start your day off right.

Every time you awaken, take a moment to stretch and enjoy your last few seconds in bed before you get up. Note that this is not the same as hitting the snooze button! Imagine this: the sun is shining, happy birds are chirping just outside your window, and for that one moment, you are seated. Bask in the moment of quiet, meditating before you contemplate everything ahead of you. The day is waiting, and you need to be on your game until you can return to your sanctum.

Every day, there are so many things to accomplish. Often, suppose we dwell upon this never-ending list. In that case, we can become overwhelmed by how much of the world needs our undivided attention. Don't let it overpower you. Think of it as a deli counter where everyone has to take a number. Whether you are part of a family or a single person, there are always responsibilities you need to shoulder. Some of these are assigned, and others you choose to take on.

You may not even be aware of your habits, whether they are considered good or bad because they have become a part of your routine. Many of your everyday routines are performed because they are easy or just plain necessary to your existence. The day's start can often include mundane tasks we perform routinely without giving them a second thought. These can be simple things like eating breakfast, brushing your teeth, or feeding your dog. Take the time you do these tasks and embrace it. Smile and think of all the things in your life you feel grateful about. We don't give our habitual actions much thought because they become a part of our daily routine.

Your morning habits influence how you think and feel for the rest of your day, so why not give yourself the best advantage you can? Take Aristotle's word for it: "We are what we repeatedly do. Excellence, then, is not an act, but a habit."

Arriving at work, you most likely brace yourself for the mayhem you are typically greeted with every morning. There is more than likely an enormous flood of emails waiting for you before you even begin your day. Your message light is probably flashing on your phone, indicating that you have at least one message. Inside, you groan. Every morning you want to get a great head start on your day. Still, you are always delayed by the avalanche of messages regularly washing across your desk.

Take a moment, breathe deeply, and set an intention for your day. Develop a calm energy before you delve into your daily routines. It's incredible how this one simple act can help you shoulder your day's tasks instead of stirring up a hornet's nest of stress.

Often, we try to make a mental checklist of what we need to accomplish that day at work and home, but what happens if we don't follow through or forget half the things we needed to do along the way? What if we start a project without the benefit of forethought, and after time spent on one train of thought, we begrudgingly figure out it wasn't quite the direction we needed to go? Now we are really stressed.

Overwhelmed, we allow ourselves to push one or more tasks to the bottom of the day's list. How often was that task the most important thing you should have done on a particular day? Instead, you skirted around it because you felt that it would be unpleasant?

Hopefully, you do not habitually choose to ignore important items on your list. But suppose you do. Are you putting your job or a promotion you want at risk? Perhaps you feel like you are sliding backward into a pool of procrastination, but how do you fix it?

Everyone knows about the drawbacks of being lured into putting tasks on the back burner because they are daunting or unpleasant. If this worries you or if you have already spiraled down the proverbial rabbit hole of procrastination, then this book is the perfect read for you. Within the following chapters, we delve into the different types of procrastinators so you can identify your behavior and formulate plans to help you along the way. Inside are proven methods to help you conquer the "put off until tomorrow" attitude.

We all know that the struggle is real when it comes to staying on top of things. You may recognize some of these actions that qualify you as a procrastinator:

- You fill your day with low-priority tasks.
- You browse several avenues of social media instead of working on that crucial task.
- If you are a student, you always put off those homework assignments.
- You promise yourself that you will start a new positive habit, but the beginning is always inconvenient.
- You're looking to start a business, but the fear of failure stops you in your tracks.
- You have a lingering to-do project or task that has been on your list for a long time.
- You read through instructions several times without making a decision regarding what action to take.
- You begin high-priority, focused tasks only to wander off and check your emails.
- You allow yourself to fill your time with unimportant tasks for others instead of tackling the most important goal of the day.
- You wait until you feel like you are in the right mood or for the "perfect time" to begin that imposing task.

We hate to be the bearer of bad news, but you are a procrastinator if you find yourself doing many of the actions above. From those examples, it's clear that the procrastination phenomenon is a complex creature.

Generally speaking, people who procrastinate do not do so intentionally. Since it is an ingrained habit, it can be tough to stop, even when you realize it is bad. It's an astonishing number, but 95% of people are chronic procrastinators. It's a terrible habit, but sometimes, it can be a sign of a serious health issue. ADHD, OCD, anxiety, stress, and depression have all been associated with procrastination. If you suspect that you are a chronic procrastinator, one of these illnesses could be to blame. Always seek out a professional's advice if you believe your habits could be attributed to these health risks.

Everyone is different, so you need to pay attention when developing a system that will work well for you. When you recognize you are habitually putting off tasks or projects, you need to regain control. Remember that procrastination can be a very debilitating habit. It can reduce self-esteem, disrupt your career, and cause you to lose your job if it is serious enough.

You are most likely experiencing a lot of frustration when researching the procrastination topic for yourself. You'll realize that many of the articles out there are partial, or their voice is too general. Perhaps you crave something more in-depth and have spent a massive amount of time surfing the internet searching for guidance. The task of reading several articles and trying to figure out what your perfect method should be is elusive. You might feel like you are drowning in an unorganized sea of information.

Within this ebook, I have provided you with a massive amount of information covering the different types of procrastinators, productivity methods, and how to get your goals on track at both work and home. If there are struggles between you and your children about procrastination, you can find ideas to strengthen your family bonds in this book.

I hope to offer practical actions and methods to use in your everyday life. While some of our content is not procrastination-specific, this particular information is related to procrastination. It can influence how we view procrastination habits and understand how those tendencies can creep into our lives. The proven methods within this book are directed toward a common objective—one that will keep you on a productive and happy path. Our goal is to help you develop constructive steps toward conquering the procrastination demon that lurks in us all.

This book is formatted to be used as a guide for reference. The choice is yours to read it straight through or skip around to the chapters you think will address your most urgent needs. It can be overwhelming to try and take in all the information represented here at once. We recommend making any notes you feel you will want to refer back to. We encourage you to read through the book as many times as you need to. There is almost always a new takeaway with each fresh read, or you may be able to change an application with a slight twist to fit your personal situation.

Your interest in this eBook has already begun your quest toward conquering procrastination. So, let the journey begin!

ONE

WHAT IS PROCRASTINATION?

The word procrastination comes from the Latin prefix pro-, meaning "in favor of", and cras-, meaning "tomorrow". No matter which dictionary you use, procrastination is defined as "to put off doing something, especially out of laziness; to postpone or delay because the task is unpleasant or boring". Ironically, procrastination is a very active process wherein we choose to do something other than the activity we should be doing.

Procrastination is hardly a new phenomenon; history shows that it has been around since circa 700-800 BCE. There have been some interesting demographic studies showing various factors surrounding procrastination. We all know that students are the most likely to procrastinate, but they are less likely to do so as people grow older.

Generally, women procrastinate less than men. There have been other studies covering demographics that also revolve around education levels and marital status. Research has even attempted to show that people exhibiting certain personality traits could have a higher tendency to procrastinate. Such as impulsiveness and negativity.

Simply put, the act of procrastination is the habit of delaying something that should have been completed on time. We tend to develop the habit of procrastinating when a task makes us feel uncomfortable. We don't realize that our mind plays tricks on us because the task's anticipation is lifted almost instantaneously by beginning the dreaded activity. Since the pain evolves from the initial resistance, we can relieve the self-imposed pressure by merely starting the task. It sounds simple, but breaking a habit is tough!

Many people often choose to wait until the time has almost run out for them to do a task. Then they merely place added pressure on themselves because of the time crunch to finish the project. In every aspect of our lives, procrastination is there, lurking, tempting us to put off until tomorrow what should have been done today.

Be it academic, health-related, or mundane chores like balancing the checkbook or cleaning out the gutters. Procrastinators find a way to put almost anything preferable in front of these chores. The habit of procrastination makes even the easiest of tasks extremely difficult.

As we mentioned, it's human nature to put some things off. Still, some people let it become such a bad habit that it eventually takes over everything they do. Some people's tomorrows are filled to the brim with tasks that they have run from in favor of. For example, playing a marathon of their favorite video game.

Perhaps today, you just don't feel that you can put in the quality work your task requires. Instead, you only reward yourself with immediate relief. Why? Because you believe the bill of goods your mind sold you. You put off the task until the next day because you are sure that you will feel more creative then.

Well, trust in the fact that you will not feel any different about it tomorrow. You can temporarily make yourself believe that a task will seem less daunting with the dawn of a new day, but when you wake up the next morning, it is still there waiting for you.

The act of procrastination can reach such chronic levels that it can begin to have adverse effects on your life. If important decisions are continually put off, it could become a problem that might cause more significant troubles.

Students are excellent examples for demonstrating various types of procrastination. Their academic tasks can become laden with such focus that they can become the elephants in the room. Students also might fear failure. That puts extra pressure on tasks until they become unbearable. All they can think about is how daunting these tasks are. They can also be less motivated to act on something in the academic world due to feeling boring. Even as a deadline approaches, they may still push an assignment aside.

Procrastinators trick themselves into thinking they are proactive and ready to work. Still, the truth is that it always ends up with them avoiding a task. A habitual procrastinator routinely postpones responsibilities until they become mentally tired, and this avoidance promotes no sense of accomplishment. It can further debilitate an individual by preying on their self-confidence. This can snowball into other complications that may begin to affect one's health, showing up as depression and sleeplessness in some cases.

The act of procrastination has been linked to many negative effects that can stifle one's very being. People who have talent but that procrastinate cannot show their true potential. How very frustrating this must feel to them to have skills that they are unable to showcase. They may begin to give up and feel a sense of hopelessness and uselessness that shakes them to their core. Riddled with conflict and indecision, a procrastinator typically does shoddy work. This is not because the task was done in a rushed manner, but because they second-guess their decisions.

We can now see that delaying or avoiding a task can trigger a rash of negativity. In turn, the procrastinator may be very unkind to themselves and begin to believe that they are a failure. Procrastinators are frequently knowledgeable people who likely put off ordinary tasks, typically because they choose to work on something more interesting. If they allow this habitual act to infiltrate their lives, they may even begin procrastinating doing meaningful work that once piqued their interests.

So, why then is it so hard to stop procrastinating? Whether your task deals with your work or is home-related, perhaps you wait until the last minute to complete it, or maybe your deadline blew past. You completely missed it, and you vow to yourself that next time will be different. However, the next time comes, and the result is the same. Why is this so?

The answer is that not all acts of procrastination have negative connotations. Sometimes, the act of procrastination can present itself as a feeling of immediate contentment. You know you have a deadline at work, but you choose to tell yourself that you will get to it later tomorrow or early next week. Suddenly, you feel a rush of relief. A kind of chemical endorphin is released in your brain. This can become very much like an addiction through which you relish in the relief you experience. Before you know it, you'll need to give yourself another dose of procrastination because, after all, the first time was such a rush. Unknowingly, we become dependent on those feelings, and we crave them, not unlike the way we might caffeine.

We can start by avoiding letting our actions define us. You

might have always been known for being late or never being able to finish a project. Well, put it in your past because there is no need to sabotage yourself continually. Start by saying no. Say no to defining yourself as a procrastinator. It is time to end the frustration and criticism by identifying yourself as having a procrastination problem. There is always a choice, so choose a new path to walk.

You may fool yourself into believing that you do your best work when you are rushed. The reality is that you may be able to do more work, but it is most likely not your best work. If you have a task in front of you and start to hedge about beginning the task, shut the behavior down right away by telling yourself no. Start now. This is probably the most demanding task of them all.

Say no to the idea of multitasking. I know that sounds counterintuitive, but multitasking is also a bad behavior and is a sneaky way to make you feel productive. Multitasking provides a false sense of productivity by making you believe that you are getting something done. Like procrastination, it lulls you into a false sense of productivity. If you notice that you are task jumping, commit to completing at least one of the activities that you are juggling.

Say no to being too comfortable. We often procrastinate because we crave being comfortable. If we avoid something that we think will not be pleasant, we trick ourselves into believing that we can take it easy and avoid a task that we dread. We must change and accept that not everything wraps us in a cocoon of seclusion and comfort.

There are four different types of procrastinators, as listed below. (We will delve into these more in Chapter 2.)
- The anxious procrastinator
- The fun procrastinator

- The "plenty of time" procrastinator
- The perfectionist procrastinator

By reading further, you will discover what category you fall into. The key to understanding why you are procrastinating in the first place will help you break the cycle you're in and rediscover the confident person you were meant to be.

TWO

REASONS FOR PROCRASTINATION

At the end of the last chapter, we dangled a bright shiny object in front of you readers that promised definitions for the four different types of procrastinators. So, it's time to begin our journey of discovery. Plunge right in; the water's fine!

Anxious Procrastinator: Our first type of procrastinator is the anxious procrastinator. This person is flooded by anxiety associated with coping with starting or completing a task or making a decision. This particular group is terrible about scheduling their time. It is often filling their available hours with more work than they can do. They worry about unrealistic expectations and deal with the stress and anxiety by procrastinating on the task.

A realistic approach to dealing with the anxious procrastinator is to use an unscheduling method. Unscheduling involves filling one's schedule with a restful slot or a fun activity for fifteen or twenty minutes at the same time every day before beginning a project. Suppose you enjoy talking with a friend, reading, playing a game on your tablet, then planning your work around that. Scheduling this downtime gives you a chance to relax, and it prevents you from over scheduling.

Fun Procrastinator: Number two on our list is fun procrastination. The fun procrastinator is the polar opposite of the anxious procrastinator. The fun type would instead do anything except the one task they need to do. Let's face it; they dread it! Now more than ever, our world is full of distractions. Given that you can do so many exciting and fun things instead of that project, it is easy to get sidetracked.

If this is your type, you already know that you will not start first thing on this questionable task. So, as an alternative, you can try to ease yourself into the activity by beginning a less objectionable task on your to-do list. While you have theoretically made your formidable task lower on your list of chores, you will still end up being productive this way. You will begin with a rewarding feeling that you have completed a task, no matter the size, and this charges up your energy so you can move forward.

"Plenty of Time" Procrastinator: The "plenty of time" procrastinator finds it difficult to start a project when the deadline seems to have an extended, drawn-out due date. This type of procrastinator is clearly a person who begins a task just a few days before its deadline. But, what if the task has no deadline? Does this task keep getting moved to the bottom of the to-do list? What if it takes weeks or even months to accomplish? It's usually something you want to do or a project that you believe will make something better in your life. However, there it is. Moved to the bottom of your list like a neglected child.

So, how do you attempt to fix this? Try setting yourself deadlines publicly. You will have advertised a commitment, and this should keep you on track and motivate you to meet your deadlines. If you feel incredibly daring, shorten the deadline a day or two just to keep yourself vested in the outcome.

Perfectionist: The last and final procrastinator is the perfectionist. The perfectionist is always striving to be the best. Often, because they criticize their own work, they never get around to starting anything, making their dreams unrealized. They envision themselves achieving the perfect job but sometimes leave it until the last minute. Thus, in effect, they permit themselves to settle for an adequate job. Above it all, they fear failure or producing a lower standard of work; they build expectations up in their minds that no one can measure up to. That can prove overwhelming. The chances are excellent that the perfectionist is already working at a high standard. Still, they have built up a higher wall of perfectionism in their mind that they must conquer.

Some feel that procrastination can be useful for the perfectionist. But how many books are never written? Music never composed? Brilliant ideas never realized? Just for the sake of the fear of imperfection? For this person, they need to reflect on their completed tasks, focus on the outcome, and determine if they were perfect. Statistically, the answer would be no. They most likely were not. This procrastinator needs to stop self-criticizing and enjoy their successes. In doing so, they will overcome their perfectionist inclinations and stop procrastinating.

Boring or Tedious Tasks

Which type of procrastinator despises boring or tedious tasks? If you guessed the fun type, then you would be correct.

Boring or tedious tasks are the number one reason people become procrastinators. Suppose the fun procrastinator even bothers with a list. In that case, the dull, time-consuming tasks will always end up at the bottom. It has proven beneficial to set a deadline for yourself for these mind-numbing endeavors. We know that it's hard to focus on the problematic, unchallenging, and monotonous tasks. However, the truth is, they still need to be completed. The fun procrastinator cannot get over how horrible the task in front of them is. They will often do anything and everything to keep from performing it.

Continue to tell yourself that it is a learning experience, and it isn't so bad or difficult. You may surprise yourself and even find that after diving into a tedious project, it turns out that it wasn't as bad as you first thought. You can always decide to give yourself a nice reward after you have finished your task, which could make it easier. Whether your task is filing a stack of paperwork, doing the taxes, or cleaning the bathroom, try making something exciting happen within the activity.

Let's take cleaning out the garage as an example. Sure, it's probably about as exciting as watching paint dry, but what if you could add a bonus? Crank up the tunes, and listen to your favorite music. It will lift your spirits, and you can make a lousy job fun; you may even complete the task more quickly, depending upon the music you choose to listen to.

Activating your imagination and creativity can turn even the most boring job into a pleasant experience. You may even find that what you thought to be the most tedious tasks suddenly have a fun and exciting factor when you just apply yourself. Also, don't forget to give yourself the reward you promised yourself upon completing your task. Not only will you look forward to finishing the task, but also, the payoff will, in turn, create a habit of being active instead of procrastinating.

Feeling Overwhelmed

Are you intimidated by a task on your to-do list? Does the thought of beginning a particular project make you feel overwhelmed? Then you, my friend, are an anxious procrastinator. You may experience anxiety, frustration, anger, shame, and even fear associated with your task. But don't run away just yet; there is hope for the anxious procrastinator!

Certainly, you would incline to get as far away from the dreaded chore as possible. It's very common to believe the built-up emotions we anticipate because they have become an ingrained habit. The very definitions of these experiences embed themselves in our minds, often developing a life of their own. We all tend to walk away from the undesirable due to the obvious negative connotations. If you work yourself up and become intimidated by a task before you even begin it, chances are that you may find that you're becoming quite cross about any deadlines associated with this task. A paralyzing fear takes over. You become more anxious, taking any opportunities you can find to hide from the task.

When you become overwhelmed, you may find that breaking the task up will be an invaluable approach. You will most likely discover the task itself is not the cause of your feelings. Indeed, it is the initial stimulus, but it is merely a catalyst for your own irrational beliefs. To help yourself move forward, you must train your mind to ignore any setbacks, such as possible mistakes. Take action to correct them in a timely fashion. Keeping this in mind, you can continue on your path and begin to place a value on your work.

Perhaps you find yourself filled with indecision as to a starting place. Often, this elusive place to begin may seem out of reach, but you must train your mind to continue moving forward. The onset can become a struggle to reach if the thought makes you initially feel paralyzed with dread. In extreme cases, you may need to seek out the help of a therapist to keep moving along on your path. They should be able to counsel you to help you identify your self-defeating habits.

Fear of Failure

Let's face it—no one likes to examine their failures. It's never a pleasant journey to take a look at our mistakes. The perfectionist procrastinator not only worries that they may not achieve success but even if they do achieve it, the idea of maintaining it is enough to send this particular procrastinator heading for the hills. A warning to those of you that are this type of procrastinator: You will probably have to do something against your brain's preferences. You will most likely have to face some failure because the more important the goal, the greater the chance of being imperfect. You will need to make your peace with this certainty and be continuously comfortable with it. Embrace the knowledge that you will still be achieving more than you imagined if you are not going to be perfect.

Without goals, you have no destination, and the only thing truly standing in your way is yourself. Take time to analyze that your fear is what is holding you back, not your abilities. The first step is to own that fact and move forward despite your trepidation. Don't obsess over the fear of not being ready for not feeling like you're good enough to handle the task. You'll find that distractions rear their ugly head every day; the trick is to avoid letting them derail your objective. Instead of blaming external forces, the perfectionist needs to recognize that they are indeed afraid and decide to change how they view their tasks.

Utilize rationality to help balance out your fears. Recognize that some amount of failure is inevitable, but the fear will often remain. Plagued by a lack of discipline, we find the clichés of 'think positively' or 'act more assertively' completely unhelpful. To face your fear of failure is not as easy as it sounds. It requires much less effort to conquer a fear of clowns or step on a crack instead of building up the fear you have created. After all, these fears, in a sense, aren't real; they are a fabricated story you cook up to appease yourself so that, in your mind, you remain "safe".

Fear of Success

Do you fear success? Many of us do without even realizing it; fear of success can often be mistaken for insecurity, so it is easy to miss. Success can be measured in many ways, such as, for instance, owning that big house, driving a flashy car, or being popular at the country club. Success looks different to everyone because of personal differences. The fear of success seems to be anchored in anxious procrastination. Still, it also maintains some aspects of the perfectionist procrastinator.

For instance, you plan out a large detailed business plan. Still, when you come down to the wire, you realize you haven't done a single thing on the checklist you so painstakingly took the time to design. This procrastination is not about lacking an actual skill. This fear announces itself to you after it's clear that you have the talent and know-how to produce the desired outcome. The worry comes not from the task itself, but your execution of it, as well as the backlash you may experience from your peers.

When you fear success, you can make yourself believe that up until now, you have just beaten the odds, riding on pure luck alone. You worry that you are not all that skilled, and this task will prove it. You might harbor deep concerns that the next big job just may reveal that all along you have been a fraud, and you worry that people will see you, not for the person you are, but who you worry you might be. While, deep down, we know that this isn't the case, it can still feel very real.

Another avenue of fearing success may be a fear you have of comparison. Perhaps you worry that you will not measure up to your idea of success nor the idea of success held by the people you admire. It is also possible that you are afraid of becoming like the successful people you have seen as abrasive, unkind, or obsessed with money. A belief that success could lead you down a path of corruption can hold you back from your dreams.

You might simply fear change. Many of us do, even without the blanket of procrastination. Becoming comfortable in your daily routines at work and home can stifle your desire to work toward change. It is simpler to settle for the comfortable way, isn't it? You may believe this to be true, but you will never overcome your procrastination habits. Because, after all, change is scary; sometimes, it can be downright terrifying.

Trying to Be Perfect

Perhaps you want to be the best at everything. Well, who doesn't? You might tend to expect a lot from yourself. Why? It is probably because you have mapped out some too high standards for yourself to meet. That's a lot of pressure for anyone to contend with, and the worst part is you have no one to blame for it but yourself. It's a self-inflicted form of perfectionist procrastination torture at it's finest. You suffer over every decision, and every hurdle you take on must end in perfection, or you fear the world will end. There is no compromise of settling for second-best. You may fool yourself into believing that you are reducing your self-induced stress by putting off a task. Still, realistically, you are putting more stress on yourself worrying about the result not living up to your expectations.

Letting go of the perception that everything you do must be perfect is an excellent start for overcoming the perfectionist's procrastination form. For many perfectionists, to give up the idea of perfectionism can lead them to chuck the whole task in the waste bin. Let's face it. If it cannot be completed perfectly, why do it? This type of thinking can rob you and often the world of some outstanding achievements. You would probably be surprised to learn that when you procrastinate less, that complete sense of panic disappears, and you end up feeling and working better. But where do you begin?

Lower your expectations. At first, this will be incredibly difficult to do, but you have to train yourself to think differently. All tasks take time, and if they end up imperfect, well, that's okay; in fact, it's normal. You must allow yourself to be human.

Laziness

The act of procrastination is often confused with the term laziness. Their meanings are very different, however. When someone is lazy, the action is described as an unwillingness to act, preferring inactivity. Procrastination is an active process of avoiding a task you should be doing, but you aren't. This type of procrastinator is known as the "plenty of time" procrastinator.

For example, let's say you have a big project you have to complete for work, but you tell yourself that you can relax because there's plenty of time. When the deadline for a task is set a long way off, this can make it difficult for this procrastinator. They lack the urgency to get started because of the perception of time. Eventually, this person typically postpones the task until that far-off deadline is suddenly tomorrow. Yikes!

Many times, the thought process surrounding this behavior is simply a lack of clarity; these individuals don't seem to be able to grasp the simple what, when, why, or how:

- What exactly is being worked on?
- How are you able to effectively do this task?
- When should you be working on this?
- Why did you need to perform this task in the first place?
- What are your priorities revolving around this task?
- When does your project need to be completed?

Suppose any of these factors seem undefined to you. In that case, you will most likely procrastinate, continually telling yourself that the task is arduous, demanding too much of your valuable energy. As a race, we are designed to preserve energy, it's second nature to avoid unpleasant situations. The alternative is much more pleasant, and suddenly we find ourselves doing something that takes less energy away from us.

It is much easier to complete a task if you keep it alive and moving rather than trying to jumpstart an immovable object that has rooted to a spot. Keep those tasks active, even if you can only devote a minimal amount of time to them each day. Anyone who has pushed a car to get it started and then ran and jumped into it will understand that it is much easier to gain momentum if you continue forward. The longer you delay, the stronger the resistance. So, get out there and move.

Uncertain Where to Start

The realization that procrastination is not a problem brought on by productivity or deadlines but rather one born from the mind is a good beginning. Start by treating yourself with kindness. Encourage yourself to apply focused strategies. To build a strong foundation, you must appreciate yourself; this way, you can overcome your imperfections. You must ask yourself why you are avoiding a task or why you dislike it so much. It's a strength to accept that you are a natural procrastinator. Never put off until tomorrow what you can do today.

Ready. Set. Begin!

THREE

USE PARKINSON'S LAW

***"Procrastination is the thief of time, collar him."–
Charles Dickens.***

If you have never heard of Parkinson's law, you are probably not alone. Cyril Northcote Parkinson, a famous British historian, and author observed after seeing how bureaucracy worked: "Work expands to fill the time available for its completion."

Have you ever wondered why your projects seem to take forever to complete? They may take a long time because you haven't set a deadline, or perhaps, you have selected a deadline, but it's so far out that the project takes on a life of its own and fills all the time you have set aside for it. Be honest: when was the last time you finished a task in less time than was given for it?

Have you ever moved from your starter home to a bigger place and then wondered how, after a while, it is filled with stuff? Just where did it all come from? It's merely the course of human nature to fill the time and space available to us. Parkinson's law has also spread to our electronics. So, now, our phone memories and hard drives are bursting at the seams because of all the photos we collect and all the websites we deem necessary to bookmark. Essentially, we have become electronic hoarders.

Parkinson's law is not procrastination, and it isn't laziness, so what exactly is it? So, here's the scoop. Parkinson's law assets that we will end up performing unnecessary work just because we have time. We justify extended deadlines by tricking ourselves into believing that the more time we allow, the better the end result will be. Instead, we fritter away most of the time in procrastination and spend only a small portion of the time on the actual project we want to complete.

Understanding the thief of time is only half the battle. In analyzing your time management perspective, you may find it to be skewed; you might notice yourself focusing on things other than the prime objective. Setting a shorter deadline can create better focus. Be reasonable with the time you allow. Remember, it is important to set limits. Any deadline is far better than no deadline at all.

Below is an elementary example of Parkinson's law:
- If you have a week to dust the house, it will take you a week to dust the house.
- If you have a month to dust the house, it will take you a month to dust the house.
- If you have six months to dust the house, it will take you six months to dust the house.
- If you have no deadline to dust the house, it most likely will never get dusted.

Wouldn't you love to get things checked off your to-do list more quickly? Everyone wants to improve their productivity. If you apply time/day constraints, it will help you change your life. There is no better feeling for a procrastinator than being able to take a big black sharpie and cross off a task.

Start by making up a detailed list of your tasks. Next, take that list of tasks and divide them up by the amount of time you will need to complete them. Now, here's the challenging part of this exercise—only give yourself half the time you allotted to achieve them. (You may need to go back and read that last line again!) Now, you will have an unbreakable deadline and a clock to race against. This exercise is extremely beneficial if you're someone who has trouble taking your deadlines to task.

Examine your tasks when they are completed and ask yourself how accurate you were setting the time constraints. You will discover that many task times will be spot on, which you may find surprising. It's even more startling when you find that other tasks may have time to spare. Of course, there will be tasks that you perhaps needed a longer time to complete. The point is that this is an exercise in judgment and how you utilize your time.

Time can be very elusive if you don't rein it in. Boundaries can help create freedom in our thinking because this forces us to have a structure from which to work. Remember that there is a distinct difference between setting a bare minimum and finding out that, suddenly, you didn't leave yourself enough time. Take care to manage your schedule effectively. You can always adjust your time constraints to accommodate needed changes. This is a learning process, so give yourself a chance.

Always keep a list of your tasks, but make sure not to overwhelm yourself. It takes a concentrated effort to keep your list shorter. A mile-long list will bring you unnecessary stress, and you will find yourself fretting over where to begin. Remember to be smart about what tasks you will include, and never put items on your list that have no deadline as, most likely, they will never get done anyway. Ensure that the most important tasks are at the top of your list and that they always have an accurate estimation of the time needed to complete them. When these are finished, you can move on to the less important activities. Make sure that you prioritize your tasks and goals by setting up a particular day of the week when you concentrate on a specific task. Take care not to set a task too far into the future (we will touch more on this later).

The more of a perfectionist you are, the more likely you are to become a victim of Parkinson's law. let's face it. The perfectionist always wants to add one more thing. They desire to tinker with their projects so they can add a new component to make it perfect. This will expand the project exponentially until all the allotted time is used. Understand what "done" means; then, own it, and resist the temptation to tweak anything.

Recognizing Parkinson's law and utilizing it to your advantage is one of the most significant changes you can make. This simple time management change will drive your focus, and you will find that you get more accomplished in the same amount of time. Your energy will escalate, and your methods will continuously improve as you discover better ways of performing your tasks.

Challenge yourself, and stay consistent. This is one of the biggest changes you can make in your approach to realizing your goals.

FOUR

EAT THE FROG FIRST

I know this chapter sounds like I am telling you what appetizer to order, but its title has nothing to do with food. Instead, it describes a productivity method that's associated with both Bill Gates and Mark Twain. Put simply. It advises you to identify one important task for the day and perform that activity first. No exceptions.

This method works wonders because we all tend to overestimate how many tasks we can achieve daily. The ability to focus on a primary goal is often lost in the day-to-day to-do lists we already struggle with, so how do we overcome this hurdle? It's easy: eat the frog first. This particular technique is perfect for establishing your productivity.

Take a look at the questions below. Did you answer yes to any?

- Do you struggle with procrastination?
- While crossing many items off your to-do list, are you still finding it challenging to complete the important tasks, pushing them off until the end of the day?

- Do you find it difficult to adhere to a productivity method?
- Is it tough for you to prioritize your work?
- Are you overwhelmed by your staggering list of things to do?

We often wonder where we failed in time management. Still, the answer is relatively simple: you didn't follow the rules of eating the frog first.

There are a couple of reasons that will cause you to fail in this method of productivity. One way is to tackle the smaller, less important jobs first, giving you a false sense of accomplishment. You believe you are moving forward when, in fact, you are falling behind. When you give in to this procrastination tactic, you might answer emails and leave the most critical task of the day for last. However, this is when your energy is at its lowest, and you have become entirely counterproductive. The lingering task will haunt you all day, draining you of life.

Even though this method promotes a consistently deep work habit, we know that our world and workplace ultimately can become more demanding in a fraction of a second. This can put our plans of eating the frog first at risk if you allow it. The ability to immerse ourselves in a distraction-free environment is not impossible. There are so many tasks banging at our doors with no regard to our already-established, lengthy list. We become preoccupied with many emails, messages, meetings, and more, often disappearing in a sea of demands. This method requires us to push back against all these distractions and focus, bringing us closer to realizing our goals.

Set your own schedule, and don't deviate from it. Everyone that comes into work checks their email and messages first, but this daily habit tends to put you in a reactive mode. The minute you have responded to these, you have compromised your time and resources. Your workday might spiral out of control since your attention has now shifted to what other people want or need you to do. You may find that your entire day was hijacked by the end of it, and your frog is still sitting there glaring at you, hungry. Eating the frog first asks you to put your schedule in front of everything else.

Don't put yourself in a position to fail; set up that win! Eating the frog first compels you to focus on less because, as we mentioned before, people tend to overestimate what they can complete in a day. Falling victim to productivity systems often gives us the impression that we are failing as we believe ourselves to be behind in our tasks. In contrast, the bad mood we begin to feel will lead us to avoid our tasks. We are instead looking for that thing that will boost our mood. Eating the frog first thing in the morning will give us that win we need to feel good and move forward.

Every hour of our workday is not created equal. Another reason to eat the frog first is that we are more productive in that first hour of work. (We hope that you have dosed yourself with a good nutritious breakfast and a jolt of caffeine; this should find you perky and ready to roll.) The method of eating the frog first utilizes your best productivity hours to complete your most challenging work. Your brain should be at its peak at this time. Frequently after lunch, a nap sounds great. But, before you curl up to slumber, now is the time to handle those less critical tasks on your list.

We have all experienced a project that took on its agenda. We swore that there was enough time to complete the task, but we eventually fell behind. How did this happen? You didn't eat the frog first. The rules follow a simple method that you can fall back on at any time. Everyone has limited daily time and energy. By eating the frog first, you're making something meaningful happen each day.

This method can prove extremely beneficial for people

who are feeling pulled in thousands of directions at once. Taking the bull by the horns and performing that one enormous task daily does not mean that once you are done, you can sit back, throw your feet up, and pop Netflix on for the rest of the day. You will still need to work on those other tasks that fill your list, but the one frog that required the most energy and attention will be accomplished. Once the urgent frog task is completed, turn your energized state into productivity.

Below you can find steps to help you map out how to eat a frog.

• First, identify your frog. This is where you determine your most difficult and important task for the day. (You can only pick one.)

• Eat it. Perform that chosen task first thing in the morning. Do not allow yourself to become distracted, putting the most important task off until later.

• Repeat this formula every day. If you consistently follow these few small steps, you may be surprised by how many significant accomplishments you can perform.

So, now you know what a frog is. The frog task is often met with mental resistance, which sets you up for (wait for it) procrastination. If your frog takes longer than four hours, you may need to break it up into smaller steps. If you need to split your task into more than two separate tasks, resist the urge to schedule your frogs for the entire week or several weeks. Setting tasks up to encompass such a large part of the future never really works out well, and you will end up falling behind or not finishing the goal at all.

Start fresh with the identification of your frog of the day. You can, if necessary, prepare which frog you will attack the night before. This timeframe will allow you to plan tasks accurately without giving mental resistance a chance to creep into your thoughts.

You may be wondering what course of action you should follow if you are not a morning person. Well, the same principles of eating the frog first can be applied to any time of day that you, as an individual, feel the most energized. The whole focus of eating the frog first is to attack your most important goals when you feel the most productive. The disadvantage to this is that you may get caught up in other tasks as your day marches on. You'll find it more difficult to break away and immerse yourself in the project you swore to take on for the day. It is important to schedule a time and stick to it—no exceptions.

What if you have more than one frog task in a day? This is not possible. You can still have priority items, but there can only be one frog. Utilizing this tool can help you overcome procrastination and bring more focus into your life.

FIVE

PRIORITIZE YOUR TASKS AND PROJECTS

To prioritize means to arrange items in order of importance or priority. In the previous chapter, we talked about how eating the frog first enables you to do the most important task before any others.

Whether at the workplace or in the home, it can be a struggle to learn how to prioritize your work. It is very distressing to overcome the "everything is important" syndrome. Mastering prioritization can reduce stress, especially when you realize that not everything is urgent. Although perfecting the best system for you can take time, it will enable you to feel in control.

We have touched on excuses people use to put things off until the last minute. Prioritization for procrastinators is the golden key to getting things done. This act arranges tasks or activities in order of their most significant importance. We need to place items that are due the same day high on the list. Other tasks might be of a high priority because they are relative to an ongoing project we are working on. So, you have to ask yourself which comes first, the important or the urgent tasks? Not to be vague, but there are usually some tasks that fit into both categories. The best avenue you can follow involves making a list of everything you need to get done. So, get out that pen and start writing.

Below, you will find two similar matrix planners that can help you plan tasks for the next day or two. Remember, as we learned in the previous chapter, planning too many days in advance can cause procrastination to seep in.

It's important to write out every task you have to complete. It doesn't matter how small they are because you should never leave tasks up to memory. Doing so opens up a whole new way to put tasks off, most likely because you will have forgotten all about them.

Task descriptions should be short but detailed. Make sure you include your deadlines because knowing when these tasks need to be completed will help you prioritize them. Fast approaching deadlines will need to be in a more urgent section. After assessing how urgent each task is, assign them a level of importance. This will help you create a schedule and keep those most time-sensitive tasks front and center.

The best time to make your list is the night before. This practice will allow you to hit the ground running first thing the following day. If something important should crop up after you have your list readied, don't worry. You already have a working list; thus, it shouldn't be too difficult to add something in. There are two trains of thought to list-making. Firstly, you have to figure out whether you are a night list person or a first-thing-in-the-morning list person. If you are a person who worries about tomorrow, and it affects your sleep, making a list the night prior might help you get that rest you need.

When designing your next day, take care to be realistic about the time a project will take and how it will affect the rest of your schedule. When you examine your to-do list, you should always make sure that the task is yours to complete. If it proves to be better handled by another, then, by all means, delegate that task to them. During this important learning experience, remember to be flexible. If you have developed that perfect schedule for the day, don't panic when something unexpected appears; it's inevitable and a good reason to build in some buffer times. This practice may prove very beneficial. It can take some time to overcome the bad habit of procrastination. Establishing a new routine is never easy, so don't give up.

Most of the information within these pages refers to work. Still, it is equally important to keep the promises you make to yourself and your family. Don't sacrifice your personal goals when you are juggling a tough list of tasks. It's very easy to put yourself last, but you need to take time for your own goals. Remember to do something fun, or build in some relaxation time.

Set Project Priorities

In addition to your matrix assignments found below, it would be prudent—especially when you are at the beginning of teaching yourself these new methods—to keep a journal of what you did. This way, you can review your plans and determine if you felt they were successful or if you thought a different approach was needed.

There are methods of time management that effectively enable you to increase productivity and fend off procrastination habits. One of these methods is called the Eisenhower Matrix.

THE EISENHOWER MATRIX UTILIZES "IMPORTANT" and "urgent" as values to help you evaluate and determine an assigned priority. With this method, you can place each task in its proper category.

- Your top priority should be given to the important and urgent tasks. (Remember that your frog is probably in this grouping.) These are tasks you need to be working on now.
- Next would be important, but not urgent tasks. These are considered to be lower priorities than the previous category. You should be comfortable performing the tasks in this category later.
- Urgent, but not important, tasks are suitable for later in the day and are typically smaller activities you can deal with quickly. Items in this box are appropriate filler tasks that can be done quickly.
- And finally, the not urgent or important tasks are to be handled as time permits. There may even be items here that can be deleted entirely once you realize how unimportant they are.

Stephen Covey developed another popular time management tool. It is a variation of the Eisenhower Matrix outlined above. This method focuses on the improvement of personal and professional relationships. Within his formula is an opportunity to develop accomplishment.

	Urgent	Not Urgent
Important	Quadrant I • Crisis • Pressing problems • Deadline-driven	Quadrant II • Relationship-building • Finding new opportunities • Long-term planning • Preventive activities • Personal growth • Recreation
Not Important	Quadrant III • Interruptions • Emails, calls, meetings • Popular activities • Pressing matters	Quadrant IV • Trivia, busywork • Time-wasters • Less important calls and emails • Pleasant activities

Important

Quadrant I
- Crisis
- Pressing problems
- Deadline-driven

Quadrant II
- Relationship-building
- Finding new opportunities
- Long-term planning
- Preventive activities
- Personal growth
- Recreation

Not Important

Quadrant III
- Interruptions
- Emails, calls, meetings
- Popular activities
- Pressing matters

Quadrant IV
- Trivia, busywork
- Time-wasters
- Less important calls and emails
- Pleasant activities

. . .

THE BENEFITS of either matrix will help you increase productivity. Having an organized and prioritized list can assist you in performing the most critical tasks promptly.

Improving your habits will begin to come more easily to you while utilizing a matrix. With them, you can focus on the more important QI and QII items. This, in turn, will enable you to find a better work-life balance.

Prioritizing tasks in this manner will help improve your planning skills and projects. Long-term goals will no longer involve tasks that have you running to the procrastination closet.

SIX

TAKE SMALL BITES

Big goals are a fact of life. They are often important but can be very imposing. One thing that fills us all with a swell of pride is to realize accomplishments and cross off tasks on our list. But what happens when we take on that massive project? It's big, huge, ginormous (did I mention it was giant?). Do you find yourself struggling with breaking tasks or projects into smaller steps? Keep in mind that a task is something that can be achieved more or less in one sitting. If you find that something will take days, weeks, or months, it qualifies as a project.

So, let's say that there is an enormous project on your to-do list. You keep staring at it, perhaps thinking the size will diminish if you give it enough time. Procrastination sets in because you feel overwhelmed each time you look at it. You feel worse about it until it grows into a behemoth instead of shrinking in size.

There is hope. We understand that it is difficult to look at that large project and wonder how you are expected to accomplish it in the world. For example, often in the reconstruction of artwork, we look at the finished piece and try to figure out how to begin; there are line drawings, gradients, and shapes, oh my! Breaking it down into layers helps you start the piece's recreation from the bottom layer up.

This application, also known as micro productivity, works at breaking a project down into smaller, more manageable "bites." This will make your goals more attainable and help lighten your mental load. Enabling you to defeat any procrastination your brain may be entertaining. Structuring your project with the small bites method produces better project management. The obvious benefit of this method is that it allows us to concentrate our full effort on smaller pieces of a project without worrying about the full-scale details. Within the smaller bites, we typically find that more attention to detail is possible. Due to breaking the project up, we can produce higher quality work. After all, as we all know, the devil is in the details.

What if you need to delegate some of the components because you do not feel qualified? The small bites method is perfect for this scenario; you will be relieved that help is on the way. A large company project means that many hands are available to help lighten the load. This process also enables you to utilize the most qualified person for each small bite.

First, identify all the things that are necessary to complete the project and clearly define them. Take the time to produce a detailed checklist. From there, you can break the project down into a group of subprojects. This process continues until the task is broken down into smaller, more manageable pieces. It is so much easier to manage a small piece than to procrastinate on a huge chunk with a glazed-over expression on your face. This can only lead to poor results.

This work structure of smaller bites is a proven method that helps us determine all the information required for our project and to have a successful outcome. The project becomes completion-friendly, and the likelihood of procrastination is reduced. This approach makes perfect sense, and as you experience how it works for you, you may wonder how you ever got anything done without this technique in the past.

It is likely that if this process is overlooked, you may find missing pieces of the project because time was not taken to plan out the details. Find yourself struggling with the project definition steps. It could be a sign that you are not familiar enough with the project and need more input. Take care and review your list to ensure that the combination of multiple steps is not compressed into a single bite.

Even the smallest part of the project may be very time-consuming. Take care to break long stretches of work into smaller sessions. This has often been referred to as "time boxing." This method adds an artificial time limit to a bite. If you need more time, add another box.

Working off a daily to-do list, you will watch as the small bites come together to form the initial realized project. You can now celebrate because the small bites method has begun to pay off.

You may ask yourself why this approach works. The human memory can be very limiting. Unless you are part of a very small percentage of people who have a photographic memory, you will find it impossible to remember everything. The average recall memory storage is typically limited to three to five tasks. If you choose to rely on your memory, the chances are excellent that you will have to come to a full stop trying to remember what the next step is. Distraction will set in, and procrastination can often take over.

Being able to mark things off your checklist can fuel your mind positively, serving as a rewards system for your brain by producing dopamine. When the brain releases dopamine, you connect to pleasurable feelings that motivate you. You might become eager as excitement builds, and you watch everything come together. The motivation you experience will keep you moving forward, seeking that next reward.

Don't limit yourself to checklists at work, either. They can be very useful in goals elsewhere. You can plan out a vacation, pack for your trip, map out a home remodeling project, or even organize a hobby/collection. The applications of the detailed checklist are endless and rewarding.

Now that your checklist is in order, you will find that you work better with specific goals. We make a conscious choice to pursue our goals, and if we stick to a list, we can exclude tangents. We are, therefore, able to increase our focus, stay persistent, and strategize. Specific goals help instigate hard work and keep us motivated. Overall, we just perform better.

There is another benefit to the large project when working on the smaller bits that are often overlooked. You have an opportunity to get feedback. You may believe that feedback is demotivating because it can contain constructive criticism. However, isn't that better than working far into a project and finding that you have drifted off course? Causing your efforts to be entirely pushed off track five bites ago? Feedback, whether positive or negative, inspires us to keep moving forward. The positive has apparent effects, such as producing long-term motivation. Still, the negative motivates us to repair our performance and try harder.

Productivity is very personal and kind of an art form. What works for one person may not work for the next. There is always going to be an individual factor that defines your tasks and projects. In the beginning, as you develop your skills, you may find you spend a considerable amount of time customizing and tweaking your productivity plans. Don't let yourself be intimidated by the size of a project.

SEVEN

WHEN SOMEONE ELSE SET YOUR DEADLINES

Self-imposed deadlines don't work for everyone, but all bets are off when someone else sets them. Under certain circumstances, you may feel like you are losing control over the entire situation. Some examples of when others set deadlines may include a term paper at school. An expected deadline for everyone in the class, or your boss may assign you a task that is to be finished by a specific date.

What concerns you about letting others set your deadlines? Are you worried that the external pressure may bring you more stress? If you miss the projected date, do you worry that others will think poorly of you because you couldn't deliver on time? What if you miss your deadline through the procrastination of others?

So, here you are, second in line. In other words, the party of the second part, you, is waiting for the party of the first part, them, to finish their section of the project before it ever reaches you. The deadline comes and goes, and still, you hear nothing. Upon investigation, you find they haven't even started yet. Now you feel stressed because you wonder how it will impact your workflow. You and perhaps your team have cleared all your tasks. Knowing that this one is due to cross your desk at any moment. Now, everyone is on hold, and that has to be frustrating.

This is more prevalent in the workplace than you might think. Even if the prior department has finished its portion of the project on time, it may be hung up in a slow approval process before it gets to you. Fearing to be included in the blame of delay for the project, you are forced to learn from your mistakes. In the future, you resolve to communicate more, trying to avoid any delay. You hope to remind the first group about the project's due date and avoid letting new tasks that might derail the long-term project until it slips through the cracks entirely.

We all know that procrastination plays a big part in not meeting a set deadline. Still, most people just aren't that excited about completing a task with others' deadline.

It's discourteous to continually set deadlines marked simply "ASAP." This can leave things open for interpretation. For the procrastinator, it can imply anything from hours to days, weeks, or even months. Thus, if you ask for help in setting deadlines or are set for you, don't be afraid to reach out and have the initiator be specific.

However, deadlines set for you don't always have to be viewed negatively. Think of those deadlines set by others as a prioritization tool that is already realized. The imposed deadline can help you focus on and assess your workload. If you know that you can make that deadline easily, then it could prove to be fun. It could give you a victory and encourage good habits.

At work, you must be honest. If you are assigned a task that you feel you were not skilled enough to do, you should let them know instead of setting an unrealistic goal for yourself. There is nothing wrong with admitting something is beyond your expertise.

If you choose to help someone set deadlines, make sure you know when the project is to be completed. The best place to put this information in writing is either in the subject line of an email or, if that is unavailable, within the first paragraph of any written details. By managing the content, you reduce the stress of the procrastinator.

A deadline is often a set date with no negotiation, but what if there is a little wiggle room? Instead of setting a specific date, perhaps begin by asking what the participators believe is a realistic timeline to complete the project. Everyone feels vested in the projects, and, in the long run, if they have helped set the deadline, they have no grounds to complain.

Here are some strategies to help keep everyone on schedule:
- Tie projects to deadlines
- Provide clear instructions
- Lead by example
- Establish constant communication
- Involve all parties in the deadline process

Deadlines should always be imposed on work that matters.

When others dictate the day's rhythm, you tend to lose control over when and how you work. This can leave you on a constant edge of interruption.

So, let's say you arrive home from work, and now it is your turn to set the deadlines. Do you have a chore chart in your home? Are you setting tasks and goals for your children?

What if your child is displaying signs of procrastination? Here, you become the one setting deadlines for others. Are there ways to help them develop better habits? We're so glad you asked! There are a few techniques for teaching your child to avoid procrastination.

One of these methods involves using two jars of similar size, placing the empty one in your child's room. The other jar you fill with pennies or spare change, and you will keep it. Every time you see your child take a task head-on, such as making their bed first thing or returning home from school and doing their homework without procrastination, drop a coin into their jar and praise them for their actions.

An additional technique involves using a visualization method. Have your child close their eyes, and tell them to picture a trip to the future. Ask them how they will feel once a task is completed and how they will feel if they don't complete the task (or even ignore it altogether). This can be a powerful tool; your child may easily be able to picture what consequences tomorrow will bring if they procrastinate.

Most importantly, though, in leading by example, your child has the best chance to grow up to become a teen who is well on their way to good time management skills. Just as you have learned that everyone makes mistakes, you must also help your child grasp this same concept. He or she must also learn to forgive themselves and be kind.

Be careful to always model good behavior yourself because procrastination is a learned habit. Your children learn best by watching you. Encourage them to take the plunge and just do it.

EIGHT

BE ACCOUNTABLE TO SOMEONE

Perhaps you are too skilled at letting yourself off the hook, and despite giving yourself a deadline, you still procrastinate and are late, or you do nothing at all. One reason could be that you fall victim to Parkinson's law, which we discussed earlier. A deadline is scheduled, but instead of taking small bites and chipping away at it to meet your goal, it whips by you at an astonishing speed. Leaving you nowhere near completion.

There is an unpopular method of making your habits of procrastination pay. Some people choose this very drastic technique that involves cause and effect. With this method, you can give a friend an envelope filled with money that would be painful to lose. Make it applicable to a task that needs to be done by a specific date and time. If you get your task done, you can have your envelope full of cash back. If you don't, you lose your money. This seems a bit over-the-top and fights against almost everything we have discussed thus far. This scenario can cause you stress and punishes you, which are the very influences we want to avoid. A better idea awaits, so read on.

Whether at work or in your personal life, you are accountable for assigned work or the responsibilities you choose to take on yourself. Accountability is an effective technique to drive performance. Besides the commitment to being accountable to someone, you must also be accountable to yourself, and you can often achieve that through an accountability partner.

Why do you need an accountability partner? Having someone to speak to can help you stay on track toward your goals. When invested with the right person, they can motivate you. Now, someone is counting on you.

This may become a more difficult task if you are a person who works alone. You may need to reach out and find someone in similar circumstances who can understand what it is like to run a business independently with no one to be accountable to. You need someone to partner up with—someone with whom you could see yourself being friends. Nothing will make you go downhill faster than trying to share projects or frustrations with someone you don't like or have nothing in common with. Hopefully, you have some common ground or at least a shared interest so that hanging out with your accountability partner will not be a painful process.

Choose someone who has a positive outlook. A negative Nancy will end up dragging you down and making you negative, too, and who needs that kind of influence? When you finish a conversation with your accountability partner, you should feel uplifted and empowered. If you feel any negativity, then you are not partnered with the right person.

This person shouldn't be your spouse. The same goes for your significant other. They may be too close to keep you accountable. It can put a strain on a relationship, causing guilt and anger to form. You should try to keep your home life separate from your accountability exercises.

Often, a person with more distance can help address your weaknesses and help you focus on the priorities at hand. Your chosen accountability partner needs to be able to call you on things and hold you accountable for them somehow. If you are not keeping your self-commitments, they need to make you aware of that in a supportive way. A partnership provides both of you support through the good and the bad. Choosing an ideal partner is essential as they can push you beyond your comfort zone. The influence of the wrong person can definitely keep you stagnant.

Qualities to look for in an accountability partner include trustworthiness, dependability, commitment, and an ability to provide you with positive reinforcement.

Getting started, you may want to schedule a call or meeting once a week or every other week to compare notes and see what is working for you and what isn't. If you cannot meet in person, there is always Zoom, or you can simply talk over the phone. The professional relationship between the two of you will only work if you are completely honest with one another about your results. In other words, don't make excuses or exaggerate. There is only one person you cheat by doing this, and that is yourself. You are not there to impress each other but to offer support and constructive comments.

Suppose the only person you have to stay accountable to is yourself. In that case, you will find it much more challenging to stay motivated. To find your accountability partner, you may have to look for them in places you wouldn't expect. Coworkers could be considered, but evaluate your friends, acquaintances, and neighbors. Think outside the box. Perhaps you could try to meet a friend of a friend, someone at a business owner's event, an individual at a chamber of commerce meeting, or even someone at your local church.

Okay, so let's say you have found the ideal person to bounce ideas off of; congratulations! Now, you have to consider how to be a good accountability buddy for them. Show up prepared to exhibit that you have given your accountability buddy serious thought, and demonstrate to them how you plan to be supportive.

Decide how to assist each other by thinking about what kind of support each of you would like to receive. This list can include some of the following ideas:

- Listening
- Providing encouragement
- Giving advice
- Showing an interest in each other's progress
- Telling each other what you need to hear, even if it's not quite what you want to hear
- Challenging each other

Throughout your communications with each other, it is vital to remember how important words are. When you begin to go over the communication rules, make sure you establish topics that might be off-limits. That adage "it's not what you say, it's how you say it" applies here. It's always good to remember that communication is key.

So, what happens when the accountability relationship isn't working? In such an instance, while you look for a suitable replacement, remind yourself that this partnership should be mutually beneficial. If you find that you are trying too hard to convince someone, move on because they're not going to be a motivating force in your life.

Be patient; the right person is out there.

NINE

REMOVE DIGITAL AND ENVIRONMENTAL DISTRACTIONS

Procrastination feeds off of distractions, and today, during our current health crisis, there are even more distractions than ever before. Many of us are currently working from home. Unless you have a quiet place or dedicated office, the normal distractions at home have increased exponentially.

Distractions are hard to ignore. We trick ourselves into believing that our distraction will only take a minute or two, which doesn't seem like it adds up too much time. These are the lies we tell ourselves. The best way to resist distracting temptations is to remove them entirely.

There is a common fear in all of us that we might miss something, but how important are those Facebook notifications? Our distractions count for a massive loss in productivity, and not all of them are electronic. A typical manager can be interrupted as often as every eight minutes. Employees can spend almost 30 percent of their time trying to get back on track after unnecessary interruptions.

So, turn off all the notifications on your phone or tablet. The only reason you need to use them is for research. You must train yourself to avoid indulging because the procrastination monster will sneak in and infiltrate your work. It is tough to resist checking your email or taking a quick peek at Amazon Prime to see what's new this week; however, it can result in loads of lost time.

Whether these distractions are more fun than what you are currently working on (let's face it, they most likely are) or just merely different, they are still appealing. And to make things worse, it has been proven that the average person who gets distracted will often take a full 25 minutes to regain their focus after the event. At that point, you have lost 45 minutes that you will never get back.

There is at least one way you can help yourself deal with distraction. You've most likely heard of a swear jar, but what if you applied this application differently? Instead of putting in a dollar every time you swore, maybe you could do this each time you perform a routine distraction. For our purposes, we will use Facebook. When you give in to the procrastination demon, and get onto Facebook, put a dollar in the jar. You may find it humorous at first, but it can help you refrain from temptations once your wallet is empty.

We thrive on instant gratification, and, sadly, most of our work doesn't provide this for us. The problem here is that we may have to wait for that work benefit somewhere in the future. Even though it may mean a lot to us, the problem is that it doesn't happen immediately.

This is the exact reason that, especially when it comes to distractions, people procrastinate more. That instant moment of fun is only one click away, and it is tough to suppress.

We need to plan ahead before we start working on those crucial tasks. So, how exactly do we go about planning our distraction-free work? First, we need to make a concerted effort to block out distractions to focus on our work.

Ready to stop procrastinating and potentially double your productivity? Just a few simple steps will make that happen for you. Remember we mentioned to eat the frog first? You need to plan your most intensive work for your most focused part of the day. Save those less important tasks for a more relaxed mode.

Ready. Set. Focus.

- Make a distraction list. This method helps you recognize all apps, games, devices, or even people that might distract you most when you are working.
- Close the door to your office. This may not be possible if you work in a cubicle, but limiting your distractions here can be possible. It's normal to organize your cubicle the way you like and bring in a bit of personalization into the mix, but don't make it a distraction.
- Set three main objectives daily. When limiting the daily number of goals, not only will you be restricting what you need to work on, but you'll find that your mind will be less apt to daydream or drift.
- Turn off those darn notifications, and put yourself in distraction-free mode. In your work environment, you need to limit those notifications. So, put emails, text messaging, and any social media like Facebook or neighborhood chat apps on hold. Once removed, these disruptions will instill a sense of calm over your workplace and enable you to focus. You do realize that notifications were designed to disrupt your focus and eat away your time, right? Remember that you can allow some messages to pop up still, so if you get an important call from a family member, you do not have to miss it.
- Unless you need it as a tool for research on the web, put the phone away. Smartphones are incredible inventions, but they are currently the number one reason for people procrasti-

nating. It reaches way past mere phone calls or text messaging because social media, Netflix, and Hay Day are all available on your phone. If you are trying to focus on an important task, put your phone in another room. Being unable to see your phone, you will have the ability to resist the temptation of grabbing it to check your messages (because you can't) quickly. This will help you focus and get more done.

- Close all tabs on your desktop that have social media on them. Close any other tabs that aren't necessary for your work, as well, and stick to it. Suppose you are unable to resist your temptations. In that case, there are website blockers that will prevent you from using social media, email, and other time-wasters for a specific block of time.
- Provide yourself with a clean work environment. People are more productive in a tidy workspace.
- Schedule your high-focus time. Everyone can only stay focused for a limited amount of time. After your scheduled block of time passes, you will need to take a break. It takes time to build up your mind to handle more extended periods of being focused. If this is a new experience, it may seem not easy at first. Still, given time, you can build your brain to handle longer periods of focusing only on your work.
- Schedule a distraction time. All those distractions we mentioned above can now be given their opportunity to shine. Schedule a short distraction time as a reward for your heavily focused block. This can be as strict or loose as you prefer. Providing yourself with this will help you manage your time and increase productivity.
- Right now, so many of us are working from home. Make sure you have a designated workplace. Distractions can creep in, so try and keep them scheduled as much as possible.
- Turn off the television. Surprisingly, people who are currently working from home believe that they can turn in

quality work even while working on it as they are watching Psych reruns.

- Take the time to prepare your workplace. If you have a complicated task ahead of you and you need to concentrate, consider emptying the wall in front of you. We all like to build our little nest of comfort, but all those photos, prints, and various knickknacks tend to make our minds wander off-topic.

A fantastic idea is to keep a procrastination log. Here you can record your obstacles and why you allowed them to set you back in focus and productivity. This way, you can refer to them, and it helps you see your patterns so you can learn from your mistakes. Below is an example chart, but you can change or add anything you wish to help you harness your procrastination monster.

Procrastinated Task	The Distraction	The Why	The Plan
Getting up early	The snooze button	I wanted to get an early start to my day, but because I stayed up too late the night before, I didn't want to get up.	Make sure that I go to bed earlier, so that I can get up on time and not start my day off in a panicked rush.
Fictional writing project	I just keep delaying, even though I have many great ideas. But I am overwhelmed by where to start.	I need to just take the plunge and get organized.	By breaking this project up into smaller pieces. Make a detailed list of each bite I need to accomplish. This will help me to not be overwhelmed by the world I want to create.
Exercise regularly	I keep putting other things first even if they are unnecessary tasks.	I keep finding other tasks that my mind tells me are more important than exercising and that I can reschedule for tomorrow.	Make a schedule and stick to it. If I plan a 15-minute workout, just do it!

TEN

FOCUS ON ONE TASK AT A TIME

Multitasking is bad. Yes, you heard that correctly. Multitasking has been proven to damage your performance and could prove harmful. Don't believe me? Read on.

Recent studies at Stanford University have shown that the brain of a multitasker could suffer irreparable damage. At first glance, we bet you think this makes zero sense, but doing more than one thing at once just means you are busier, not more productive.

We have our modern workplace to blame for the root problem of multitasking. The daily pressures overwhelm us, causing us stress. The recipe for disaster was born in the workplace. When you put these together, it's no wonder we try to multitask.

Here are some reasons why this is so:
- There is always too much to do.
- No clear priorities are set, or everything is given the same importance.
- Too much time is spent with emails, meetings, and chat.
- You struggle in a distracting work environment.

People inundated with several forms of electronic information cannot pay attention or control their memory. Stanford researchers have found that those who prefer to complete one task at a time are more productive than their counterparts.

Have you been emailing or instant messaging while watching television and possibly working on a school paper all at the same time? To paraphrase a quote from Scotty in the Star Trek movie from 2009, "The notion is like trying to hit a bullet with a smaller bullet, while wearing a blindfold, riding a horse."

It has long been assumed that a person should not process more than one type of information at a time. The very act seems impossible. A select few people out there appear to handle multitasking well. Researchers have guessed that they must have excellent control over their thought processes. They can filter out irrelevant information. Overall, most multitaskers tested out as poorly in performance as the single task performers.

If, up until now, you've been a multitasker, you may find that the practice of a single task approach will be less stimulating. It's hard for the multitasker to let go of the incredible feeling they receive from believing they are multitasking. Since it is impossible to focus on more than one task, we now know that the multitasker brain is rapidly switching between two or more tasks. Multitaskers spread their focus too thin, ending up doing a mediocre job at everything. Retraining yourself in this habit will be a challenge at first, but you will find that the rewards will allow you to do better and be better.

The three main ingredients of productivity are time, energy, and attention. The single task approach allows you to focus more attention on your work. In turn, you can devote more profound attention to a task and work more creatively.

So, you want to change your habits, but you don't know how to begin. Well, we have some tips for you:

- Try to focus on the creative or more difficult tasks first. Since many of our tasks are often mindless, we find it difficult to switch gears and suddenly be creative. A daily list of making decisions will wear out your brain, and you will have a challenge focusing on the more demanding tasks.
- Break up your work to stay focused. Change things up, especially if you are working from home. Change locations to refresh your brain.
- Treat your mind as if you were training a muscle. Practice concentration by ridding yourself of distractions and focusing all of your attention on that one thing. Start with smaller increments of time, and work your way up.
- Utilize noise-canceling headphones while working. Make the world disappear, even for a bit. Distractions don't even have to be directed at you; it could be someone merely having a conversation near you.
- Write yourself reminders. It doesn't matter if you have just started on the focused journey or are driving somewhere and an epiphany strikes; keep reminders in a frequently used area like on the refrigerator or the door heading into the garage.
- Finding the right place to work is a brilliant idea to avoid distractions. This has to be a location where you can stay focused.
- Understand that emotional distractions can suddenly pop up out of nowhere, and they are one of the worst things you'll have to deal with. Put them out of your mind.
- Simplifying your life can help you on your journey. Many of us are so preoccupied with tasks that we really don't need to do. Learn to recognize these tasks and then stop doing them.
- Meditation before work can be very rewarding. This doesn't mean that you have to perform yoga before work (although that's okay, too). Meditation can be anything that

helps calm you and removes all unpleasant thoughts from your day.

- Get in some exercise. It helps to break away from your computerized world and take a walk or do something physical. If you work from home and it's lunchtime, grab Scruffy and go for a walk around the block.
- A healthy snack can help power up your brain. Fruits, trail mix, or plain nuts are great alternatives to greasy potato chips or sugary candy bars.
- Don't forget to celebrate. For just a moment, pat yourself on the back after completing a task. That first duty of the day is done, and you managed to stay on target. Treating yourself is important. Focusing is really hard work.

When we concentrate on one task, it helps us build our attention span, enabling us to control our direction. If you still don't believe this is true, give yourself a test next week, and try a single task method. Pick a task, and focus on it for 20 minutes. Don't deviate, but experiment and channel your focus on just one activity. Your brain may rebel at first, but afterward, you will feel extraordinary.

Focusing on one thing at a time will take less energy, and there will be less stress involved with the task. You will develop better productivity as you retrain your mind and create a flow. We often fail because we lack the concentration needed to devote to one project. Have you ever wondered why some days drag by while others seem to disappear in the blink of an eye? It has to do with the single task and the flow surrounding it. By practicing the single task, you can continue to push your skills beyond your current parameters, ultimately becoming more skilled. It's ironic when you think about it—we get more done by slowing down.

So, why is flow so elusive? Frankly, most work environments stifle the pursuit of flow. The busywork that fills our days has made the art of flow problematic. The pace set inside the workplace flows into our everyday life, making it almost impossible to focus on a single-minded goal. Finding your flow takes practice, patience, and discipline. If you can find it, you will be up to 500 times more productive than when you are struggling with multitasking. Yes, you read that correctly—500 times more productive!

Becoming more creative is a bonus side-effect of a single task. People may trick themselves into believing that a single task will prove to be incredibly dull over a long period, but the reverse is actually true. Digging deeper will enable you to develop aspects you never thought of before (a creativity booster, if you will).

Successful people work on one thing at a time. So, do one thing at a time, and do it well.

ELEVEN

INCENTIVES TO GIVE YOURSELF

When you reward desired behavior, it gets repeated.

Suppose you start out training your puppy to shake hands. In that case, you begin by holding your outstretched hand and grasping their paw lightly, and you follow it up by giving them a treat and telling them they are a good boy or girl. After a few times, your family dog has learned that holding out their paw provides them with a treat and praise.

This is a very simplistic but accurate example of how behavior works. If we receive a reward for good behavior, we will gladly repeat it. We can form good habits in precisely the same way. When your brain recognizes the pattern of a reward system, the habit kicks in automatically.

By using rewards and psychology, you can train yourself to procrastinate less and be more productive. According to Neil Fiore, the procrastination expert who authored The Now Habit asserts that the one main reason people seek out procrastination is that it rewards them with temporary relief from stress.

The problem with a habitual procrastinator is that there is

no good behavior to reward. They have already put their task off by watching TV, playing video games, surfing social media, and running out for a specialty coffee. This kind of person is rewarding themselves for procrastination. In a strange twist, the habitual procrastinator is usually unlikely to reward themselves for a job well done. This is probably because they have already been rewarding themselves, so they feel that they do not deserve it.

So, procrastinators reward themselves for procrastinating while never rewarding themselves for good behavior or habits. They exist in a paradox, and there is no real incentive to change. This is also how addictions work.

There is a way to correct this unwanted behavior. It is the simple two-step process that is outlined below:

1. Don't beat yourself up for procrastinating.
2. Reward yourself if you don't procrastinate.

You can overcome procrastination using willpower and strength. Since self-criticism is often a product of procrastination, it can cause some significant roadblocks concerning progress toward your goals. Remember to forgive yourself after an act of procrastination. This will lead to less procrastination during the pursuit of future goals.

You already want to overcome this habit by reading this book. Thus, we know that you have that inner strength to begin the road to better behavior. Start by praising yourself for even the smallest improvement. After you start your journey to defeat procrastination, treat yourself every single time you get something done without the bad behavior. It doesn't matter if the task is big or small. Offer yourself that reward. When you praise yourself for making the right decisions, you gain more strength. Reinforce the behavior you want, and repeat it as often as the desired action is performed. You will begin to find that you are following through more, and you will start feeling better about yourself.

It sounds daunting, but you must practice the art of self-praise. Make sure that you always catch yourself when performing correctly. When you train your animals, you offer them over-the-top praise for a correct act, so why should you treat yourself differently? Be your own cheerleader, and take the time to celebrate your good behavior.

Take the time to write down your wins, no matter how big or small. This works especially well right before bedtime because you can close your eyes knowing you have experienced a few wins for the day. You can sleep easy knowing you are making progress. Jot down a side note to acknowledge what went well, so you can look back upon it and reflect. At this juncture, you must celebrate the good behavior you desire. Don't overlook the reward, even if you believe the task is too insignificant to acknowledge.

In the beginning, we need to seek gratification rewards that will substitute our longer reward goals. So, while you want to invest in yourself by using meditation or good nutrition/better health, it may be better to reward yourself with an episode of your favorite TV series. When you complete a big work project, celebrate with a nice night out, or buy that outfit, you have had your eye on for weeks.

The event and the follow-up reward cycle will become a learned habit. Instead of treating yourself as a procrastinator, you are now rewarding yourself for finishing tasks and productive efforts.

TWELVE

PERFORM A WEEKLY CHECKUP OF YOUR GOALS

As with any change in habits, it is important to keep checking on your progress. A few points to cover weekly may include the items in the list below:

- Did you experience any difficulties in achieving your objectives this week? If so, what did you do to overcome them, or did you overcome them?
- What are your priorities for next week, and do they require any preplanning?
- Are there challenges that you face week after week that you need a better solution for?
- What's going well for you? What isn't working for you?

Most of us participate in a ritual commonly known as the New Year's resolution. Those who participate decide what they want to accomplish in the year to come. (Wow, that's a lot of space for procrastination to set in.) Only a tiny percentage of participants achieve their goal; most frankly, they don't make it past the first week of January before giving up altogether.

We previously mentioned not to give in to the temptation to set your goals too far in advance because you give yourself an open door for procrastination. But just because you may or may not have a long-term plan, remember that those big goals and projects can be broken down into smaller portions. Take care to keep that laundry list of components, but don't schedule them too far out into the future. Whether that piece will be your daily frog or not, remember to use your matrix tables and schedule the most urgent and important tasks first.

There are some very lofty goals out there. It may be time for you to grab the brass ring. If you change your tactics and develop a plan, this year could be the one. So, set those goals and go forth and conquer.

Focus on the process, and ignore the outcome. We know that it's very tempting to set those milestone goals. We all have them, and they can include losing weight, writing a book, studying to develop a new skill, or saving for retirement. Instead, fine-tune your list. Take more walks. Write 1,000 words every day starting at 9 am. spend an hour every evening reading up on your new skill interest. Or make up a special fund to put away 20 dollars a week. Large outcomes can motivate you, but focusing on the process helps you achieve those long-term achievements.

You can use a planner to keep track of your weekly goals. Picture those signs at work that say "90 days without an accident". Use your planner in the same manner. Check off each day that you complete your daily goal. If you can continue to do this every day, you will have an unbroken chain of days. It's a relatively straightforward tactic, but built up over weeks, you will find you are hooked on making progress with so many checked off days to show for it. Who wants to go back to zero days with no goals realized?

You can use a chart to help you review every week:

Week: _____

Event	Thoughts	Feeling	Evaluation	Change
Walk around the block every day	This is relaxing and allows me to meditate before I start my workday.	Enjoying being outside.	Continue the act.	Perhaps add a second, longer walk in the early evening.
Write 1,000 words every day at 8 am.	Some mornings, I find it difficult to concentrate because I know I have a lot on my plate on any given day.	Mostly positive, but I feel that I need to add something calming before I start my daily block.	Changing the order of my morning routine may help me stop struggling.	Maybe I should schedule Sammy and Anna's feeding before I try to write instead of before I go to work.
Put away $20 every week	Putting this in writing helps me to realize my goal, and it becomes easier.	After several weeks, I can see my fund growing, and I feel positive that I am achieving my goal.	Continue the act.	If I can get a bill or two paid off, perhaps I can dedicate a little bit more weekly to my fund.

Reviewing your performance weekly will help you see your progress. Remember that aiming for goals, especially long-term ones, is hard work. You can also use this weekly check when meeting with your accountability partner. Compare notes, and get feedback concerning how you are both doing. Remember that it isn't a competition. Offer constructive comments on how your partner might improve their weekly analysis.

Weekly checks are a great motivation to do better. Whether at home, meeting with your accountability partner, or in the workplace, these reviews will let you know that you are on the right track. Often, all that it takes to motivate someone is giving them a little feedback. The correct attention to your efforts will make you feel valued and improve your skills. With your accountability partner, you are already getting together weekly, so this should easily be covered within your meeting.

Suppose your workplace doesn't participate like this. In that case, it might be a good idea for you to bring it up in a weekly meeting or drop it in the proverbial suggestion box. One-on-one meetings between managers and employees improve skills on both ends. Besides the noticeable impact, this will have on communication skills, managers will learn better leadership, and employees will become better problem solvers.

If this is a new concept to your workplace, make sure they understand how beneficial this practice will be for them. As an organization, they will be able to improve productivity.

Workplaces often make the mistake of only having the bosses tell the employees what to do. A weekly check-in allows assessing how the employee is doing and permits them to express their concerns. Bosses do not have to feel like this will be a massive time-waster because they dread long, drawn-out meetings. In actuality, these meetings should be short and private. They remove stress and make productivity soar. Give your employee/boss your full attention. Be respectful, and leave your phone alone (or better yet, leave it at your desk).

THIRTEEN

DON'T BE HARD ON YOURSELF IF YOU FAIL

No matter what our work or life revolves around, we all get stuck at one time or another. Everyone suffers from setbacks and failures. Sometimes, we convince ourselves that all our hopes and dreams are lost because of our failures. This action, above all others, is hardest on the perfectionists. They are the kind of people who will continue to criticize themselves long after a mistake has been corrected. We are going to tell you right now that it's okay to fail. We are typically much harder on ourselves about our failures than others around us.

Whether you suffer from writer's block or your project has hit a creative dead-end, now is the time that you may be allowing negative self-talk to appear on your doorstep. Perhaps you try to convince yourself that your idea wasn't any good in the first place. You keep constantly disappointing yourself because you believe you should be better at whatever task this is by now.

If we give in to the shame we feel, we enter an uncomfortable habit of self-criticism. This is where we can cause destructive events simply because we are too hard on ourselves. We should want to avoid the self-infliction of anxiety, depression, substance abuse, and the projection of a negative self-image. All of these things decrease not only your motivation but also your self-worth. Give the gift of self-compassion, and make it a habit to be kind to yourself. In a strange twist of an adage, do unto yourself as you would do unto others.

Because we tend to feel shame and guilt over failures or roadblocks, we need to resist the temptation to continue this action until it develops into a chronic problem. These negative emotions are distracting and tend to make us seek out a "feel good" activity. So, we break out the butter pecan ice cream with extra praline topping while scrolling through Facebook looking for some funny videos of cats. There goes your productivity and, with that, in marches procrastination.

We all need to be aware when this behavior starts happening and be ready with a helpful alternative that won't distract us. We need to keep ourselves on track. Redirection of the negative will help you produce useful rephrasing. Instead of spiraling, thinking the whole idea wasn't a good one in the first place, change it to reflect that only this transition is causing you issues. You can still believe in the goal of the project as a whole. This will keep you in a more positive state of mind. If you are disappointed in your learning curve and feel that you should be better by now, just recognize that every project will differ. Making the parameters is always going to be a new process. We have been and will continue to be our own worst critics.

Our lack of self-confidence can make us suffer emotionally and mentally. Frequently, we read negatively into vague statements made by others. We suffer until the time we find out that it wasn't meant as a criticism; then, we breathe a sigh of relief. This is a negative default reaction.

Face it. There will be at least one time in your life when

you are going to fail at something. You can have immeasurable talent, intelligence, great work ethics. A huge four-leaf clover under your support arches every day, ending in a y, but failure is inevitable. Even though some will refuse to admit it, everybody fails. Research some of the most successful people throughout history, whose failure prompted their success story. J.K. Rowling, Walt Disney, and Steven Spielberg are all examples of failure before success. Just take a look at what they went on to accomplish. We are in good company!

While it's true that you learn more from failure than success, you will never be able to ascertain which areas you need to improve upon without the experience of failure. When actions or tasks are brought to your attention that you have done incorrectly, this is meant to help you, not hurt you.

Failure makes you stronger. Strong people will embrace their failure, and from it, they will gain incredible strength. This is what it should do for you. When others fail, they will give up on their goals and dreams, but you shouldn't let yourself be one of these people. Don't let failure stop you from your ambitions. We only get one chance to realize our dreams, so trust in yourself.

Have you ever met someone afraid to fail? They are pretty dull, aren't they? You will notice they always play it safe and never take any chances. Then, there is the rest of us. Have you ever applied for a big-time job, even if you don't meet all the requirements? These are actions that make life more enjoyable. These risks may seem frivolous, but they build confidence, making you less afraid.

Failure can follow you down a career path and, all of a sudden, you may realize that you have been on the wrong road all this time. This forces you to seek out a new path that you have never considered. Without failure, you would have continued traveling in the wrong direction.

You can never really enjoy success to its fullest until you have failed. To succeed after one or several failed attempts can make a triumph that much sweeter.

Below, find some powerful ideas on how to quit punishing yourself for a failure:

- Mistakes are all part of learning.
- Don't obsess over your mistakes.
- Commit to self-kindness. Try letting go of self-judgment.
- If you find yourself spiraling into negativity, try focusing your energy on something you care about. Volunteer to walk shelter dogs, run errands for an elderly family member, show a veteran with PTSD that someone still cares, or work at a senior volunteer organization. Just pick something near and dear to your heart that you value.
- Never compare yourself to others. The only person you are allowed to compete with is yourself.
- There is no right way that's stamped in stone to do anything.
- Don't let people who criticize you define you. Let their words inspire you to try harder.
- Accept your weaknesses. Everyone has them, and no one is good at everything.
- Don't underestimate your talents.
- Stay positive, and take care of yourself.
- Only hang out with people who want to see you succeed. This should be common sense, because who wants to be friends with the kind of people who are just waiting for you to fall on your face?
- Make an effort to recognize the difference between your self-critical state and how you feel once you let go of negative self-criticism.

CONCLUSION

Throughout this ebook, you have received some powerful knowledge to help you defeat your procrastination habits. Suggestions have been made to help you increase your productivity and suppress the natural urge to procrastinate. Where possible, we have supplied you with examples you can use in your everyday life to defeat your habitual procrastination.

We have helped you understand how and why you procrastinate. The different types of procrastinators have been reviewed in detail so that you can better understand which category you fit into based upon your history of procrastination.

Different rationalizations surround your procrastination habits, and we have taken the time to explain them. We have also provided you with unique tools and insight to beat your inclination to procrastinate.

The powerful suggestions within these pages will help you make changes to your life for the better. No longer will you allow procrastination to creep into your thoughts. You will be able to live life to the fullest, be healthy, and be happy instead of giving in to your fears or running from responsibilities.

CONCLUSION

You will be able to erase negative thoughts and emotions from your mind. Because you have been given detailed steps to reward yourself when you perform good habits, you will no longer flood your mind with self-criticism and negativity. Now, you can embrace your future and look forward to new challenges. You have worked hard and deserve the new outlook you have gifted yourself. Make sure you celebrate!

Yesterday, you put off a task until tomorrow because you didn't feel up to it, or you didn't feel creative enough to pull off the end result satisfactorily. Now, look out; here comes tomorrow, and you probably wished it had never come. You have now most likely realized that you feel the same way about the task today as you did yesterday.

Hopefully, you have realized that getting started is the key to relieving the anticipation you experience with a task. The immediate release of good endorphins when you begin your task should enforce this observation. Getting started on the activity will increase your confidence, motivation, and optimism, promoting happiness. These endorphin-promoted feelings will replace the self-criticism, doubts, and worry that have plagued you when you've allowed procrastination to influence your decisions.

Big projects that have always seemed so overwhelming in the past can now be taken in stride by learning how to break them into small bites. Instead of losing focus within the project, you can stay on track by writing out each step in a detailed fashion to not become sidetracked. Your project will be completed through delegation and careful planning in a timely manner, and your productivity will grow.

Start your most focused part of the day with the most urgent and essential task you have taken to pinpoint. You have learned by reading this book that the day's big focus should be tackled when you feel the most energized. This leaves smaller

CONCLUSION 71

tasks to fill in the rest of your day based upon importance and urgency.

Understanding prioritization through charts and lists will help guide you to better organizational habits and fend off procrastination. Through the utilization of these tools, you have learned how best to organize your day, break down large projects, and dismiss tasks that you don't need to do.

Keeping a journal helps you identify a task through steps. Did you procrastinate, and why? When you performed the task, how did you feel about the outcome? Was it successful or, upon reflection, could you have done something differently to make it better? You can also utilize a procrastination log, at which point you can review avoided tasks. The reason or distraction that caused avoidance. Your plan going forward to prevent a repetition of the action. Next time, you should record a success.

Don't reward yourself for procrastination. Sure, we are all tempted to check emails or social media more than we should, but try your best to avoid giving in to the digital demon. Only absorb those habits that make you stronger.

A reward system helps us create positive, productive habits. Working in small increments, we can re-train ourselves with how we process and complete tasks. Remembering to reward even the smallest achievement will boost our morale and self-confidence.

You have learned that you do not have to be in this alone. There are others out there in similar circumstances. Finding the right accountability partner will prove beneficial to you both. Being able to bounce thoughts and outcomes off an equal will help guide each other to better understanding and productivity.

Kindness goes a long way, but often, we forget to be kind and forgiving to ourselves. Torturing yourself over a project gone astray will lead to more procrastination in the future. Remember that everyone fails, and we need to accept this as fact; every person suffers setbacks. The key takeaway is not to give up. To fail makes us stronger.

Monitor your progress. A frequent check of your events and evaluations for a given week can help you form future plans of success, monitor your feelings, and offer observations that may include changes in your processes.

We have given you suggestions on how to remove distractions from your environment. Many influences out there fighting for your time. Our strategies help you handle the temptations that infiltrate your everyday life.

Take care of yourself. People fall into the procrastination routine because they don't support themselves. Eat right, schedule exercise, and get plenty of sleep. This may sound like common sense, but since lacking energy is one of the leading causes of procrastination, these seem like reasonable requests to help you form a better work habit.

Don't forget to schedule in some fun. Your to-do list should not only be filled with work and chores. Giving yourself a pause is also essential, not only for your mental health but also to provide yourself with one of those little rewards we recommended several times. No one is asking you to give up your favorite television show. I am only trying to convey to you that it should be a reward after a task.

Remember to meditate. Scheduling in quiet time helps calm the mind and, therefore, you're able to focus on your task when you return to it.

Your end game should be to live a disciplined life. Take your pup for scheduled walks, read books, and eat healthily. Living a scheduled life is the key to self-control. Our procrastination-free standards should be user-friendly. Don't think you need to meditate for 30 minutes; settle on 2 or 3. You don't need a 60-minute, intense workout; do your activity for just a fraction of that time, like, for example, performing a quick movement on an exercise ball.

It can take time to overcome a bad habit. Start small, establish a new routine, and watch your life improve. Don't give up!

REFERENCES

Bradberry, T. (2014). Multitasking Damages Your Brain and Career, New Studies Suggest. Forbes. [online] Available at: http://www.forbes.com/sites/travisbradberry/2014/10/08/multitasking-damages-your-brain-and-career-new-studies-suggest/amp/.

Covey, S.R. (2013). 7 Habits Of Highly Effective People. Simon & Schuster Ltd.

Fiore, N.A. (2007). The Now Habit: a strategic program for overcoming procrastination and enjoying guilt-free play. Penguin Putnam.

Steel, P. (2010). The procrastination equation: using motivational science to maximize your health, wealth, and happiness. Harpercollins.

Star Trek. (2009). [film, dvd] paramount.

Tracy, B. (2017). Eat that frog!: 21 great ways to stop procrastinating and get more done in less time. ebook ed. London: Yellow Kite, An Imprint Of Hodder & Stoughton.

ABOUT THE AUTHOR

Monique Joiner Siedlak is a writer, witch, and warrior on a mission to awaken people to their greatest potential through the power of storytelling infused with mysticism, modern paganism, and new age spirituality. At the young age of 12, she began rigorously studying the fascinating philosophy of Wicca. By the time she was 20, she was self-initiated into the craft, and hasn't looked back ever since. To this day, she has authored over 40 books pertaining to the magick and mysteries of life.

To find out more about Monique Joiner Siedlak artistically, spiritually, and personally, feel free to visit her **official website**.

www.mojosiedlak.com

- facebook.com/mojosiedlak
- twitter.com/mojosiedlak
- instagram.com/mojosiedlak
- pinterest.com/mojosiedlak
- bookbub.com/authors/monique-joiner-siedlak

OTHER SERIES BY MONIQUE

African Magic
Hoodoo
Seven African Powers: The Orishas
Cooking for the Orishas
Lucumi: The Ways of Santeria
Voodoo of Louisiana
Haitian Vodou
Orishas of Trinidad
Connecting With Your Ancestors

Practical Magick
Wiccan Basics
Candle Magick
Wiccan Spells
Love Spells
Abundance Spells
Herb Magick
Moon Magick
Creating Your Own Spells

Gypsy Magic
Protection Magick
Celtic Magick

Personal and Self Development

Creative Visualization
Astral Projection for Beginners
Meditation for Beginners
Reiki for Beginners
Manifesting With the Law of Attraction
Stress Management
Being an Empath Today

The Yoga Collective

Yoga for Beginners
Yoga for Stress
Yoga for Back Pain
Yoga for Weight Loss
Yoga for Flexibility
Yoga for Advanced Beginners
Yoga for Fitness
Yoga for Runners
Yoga for Energy
Yoga for Your Sex Life
Yoga: To Beat Depression and Anxiety
Yoga for Menstruation
Yoga to Detox Your Body
Yoga to Tone Your Body

A Natural Beautiful You

Creating Your Own Body Butter
Creating Your Own Body Scrub
Creating Your Own Body Spray

Last Chance Join My Newsletter!

If you missed it, I have a free gift available for you and wanted to remind you it's still available.

mojosiedlak.com/self-help-and-yoga-newsletter

Thank you for reading my book.
I really appreciate all your feedback and would love to hear what you have to say! Please leave your review at your favorite retailer!

www.ingramcontent.com/pod-product-compliance
Lightning Source LLC
Chambersburg PA
CBHW071311040426
42444CB00009B/1968